GUESTS

NAME AND RELATIONSHIP TO PARENTS

_____

_____

ADVICE FOR PARENTS

_____

_____

_____

WISHES FOR BABY

_____

_____

_____

GUESTS

NAME AND RELATIONSHIP TO PARENTS

_____

_____

ADVICE FOR PARENTS

_____

_____

_____

WISHES FOR BABY

_____

_____

_____

GUESTS

NAME AND RELATIONSHIP TO PARENTS

_____

_____

ADVICE FOR PARENTS

_____

_____

_____

WISHES FOR BABY

_____

_____

_____

GUESTS

NAME AND RELATIONSHIP TO PARENTS

_____

_____

ADVICE FOR PARENTS

_____

_____

_____

WISHES FOR BABY

_____

_____

_____

GUESTS

NAME AND RELATIONSHIP TO PARENTS

_____

_____

ADVICE FOR PARENTS

_____

_____

_____

WISHES FOR BABY

_____

_____

_____

GUESTS

NAME AND RELATIONSHIP TO PARENTS

_____

_____

ADVICE FOR PARENTS

_____

_____

_____

WISHES FOR BABY

_____

_____

_____

GUESTS

NAME AND RELATIONSHIP TO PARENTS

_____

_____

ADVICE FOR PARENTS

_____

_____

_____

WISHES FOR BABY

_____

_____

_____

GUESTS

NAME AND RELATIONSHIP TO PARENTS

_____

_____

ADVICE FOR PARENTS

_____

_____

_____

WISHES FOR BABY

_____

_____

_____

GUESTS

NAME AND RELATIONSHIP TO PARENTS

_____

_____

ADVICE FOR PARENTS

_____

_____

_____

WISHES FOR BABY

_____

_____

_____

GUESTS

NAME AND RELATIONSHIP TO PARENTS

_____

_____

ADVICE FOR PARENTS

_____

_____

_____

WISHES FOR BABY

_____

_____

_____

GUESTS

NAME AND RELATIONSHIP TO PARENTS

_____

_____

ADVICE FOR PARENTS

_____

_____

_____

WISHES FOR BABY

_____

_____

_____

GUESTS

NAME AND RELATIONSHIP TO PARENTS

_____

_____

ADVICE FOR PARENTS

_____

_____

_____

WISHES FOR BABY

_____

_____

_____

GUESTS

NAME AND RELATIONSHIP TO PARENTS

_____

_____

ADVICE FOR PARENTS

_____

_____

_____

WISHES FOR BABY

_____

_____

_____

GUESTS

NAME AND RELATIONSHIP TO PARENTS

_____

_____

ADVICE FOR PARENTS

_____

_____

_____

WISHES FOR BABY

_____

_____

_____

GUESTS

NAME AND RELATIONSHIP TO PARENTS

_____

_____

ADVICE FOR PARENTS

_____

_____

_____

WISHES FOR BABY

_____

_____

_____

GUESTS

NAME AND RELATIONSHIP TO PARENTS

_____

_____

ADVICE FOR PARENTS

_____

_____

_____

WISHES FOR BABY

_____

_____

_____

GUESTS

NAME AND RELATIONSHIP TO PARENTS

_____

_____

ADVICE FOR PARENTS

_____

_____

_____

WISHES FOR BABY

_____

_____

_____

GUESTS

NAME AND RELATIONSHIP TO PARENTS

_____

_____

ADVICE FOR PARENTS

_____

_____

_____

WISHES FOR BABY

_____

_____

_____

GUESTS

NAME AND RELATIONSHIP TO PARENTS

_____

_____

ADVICE FOR PARENTS

_____

_____

_____

WISHES FOR BABY

_____

_____

_____

GUESTS

NAME AND RELATIONSHIP TO PARENTS

_____

_____

ADVICE FOR PARENTS

_____

_____

_____

WISHES FOR BABY

_____

_____

_____

GUESTS

NAME AND RELATIONSHIP TO PARENTS

_____

_____

ADVICE FOR PARENTS

_____

_____

_____

WISHES FOR BABY

_____

_____

_____

GUESTS

NAME AND RELATIONSHIP TO PARENTS

_____

_____

ADVICE FOR PARENTS

_____

_____

_____

WISHES FOR BABY

_____

_____

_____

GUESTS

NAME AND RELATIONSHIP TO PARENTS

_____

_____

ADVICE FOR PARENTS

_____

_____

_____

WISHES FOR BABY

_____

_____

_____

GUESTS

NAME AND RELATIONSHIP TO PARENTS

_____

_____

ADVICE FOR PARENTS

_____

_____

_____

WISHES FOR BABY

_____

_____

_____

GUESTS

NAME AND RELATIONSHIP TO PARENTS

_____

_____

ADVICE FOR PARENTS

_____

_____

_____

WISHES FOR BABY

_____

_____

_____

GUESTS

NAME AND RELATIONSHIP TO PARENTS

_____

_____

ADVICE FOR PARENTS

_____

_____

_____

WISHES FOR BABY

_____

_____

_____

GUESTS

NAME AND RELATIONSHIP TO PARENTS

_____

_____

ADVICE FOR PARENTS

_____

_____

_____

WISHES FOR BABY

_____

_____

_____

GUESTS

NAME AND RELATIONSHIP TO PARENTS

_____

_____

ADVICE FOR PARENTS

_____

_____

_____

WISHES FOR BABY

_____

_____

_____

GUESTS

NAME AND RELATIONSHIP TO PARENTS

_____

_____

ADVICE FOR PARENTS

_____

_____

_____

WISHES FOR BABY

_____

_____

_____

GUESTS

NAME AND RELATIONSHIP TO PARENTS

_____

_____

ADVICE FOR PARENTS

_____

_____

_____

WISHES FOR BABY

_____

_____

_____

GUESTS

NAME AND RELATIONSHIP TO PARENTS

_____

_____

ADVICE FOR PARENTS

_____

_____

_____

WISHES FOR BABY

_____

_____

_____

GUESTS

NAME AND RELATIONSHIP TO PARENTS

_____

_____

ADVICE FOR PARENTS

_____

_____

_____

WISHES FOR BABY

_____

_____

_____

GUESTS

NAME AND RELATIONSHIP TO PARENTS

_____

_____

ADVICE FOR PARENTS

_____

_____

_____

WISHES FOR BABY

_____

_____

_____

GUESTS

NAME AND RELATIONSHIP TO PARENTS

_____

_____

ADVICE FOR PARENTS

_____

_____

_____

WISHES FOR BABY

_____

_____

_____

GUESTS

NAME AND RELATIONSHIP TO PARENTS

_____

_____

ADVICE FOR PARENTS

_____

_____

_____

WISHES FOR BABY

_____

_____

_____

GUESTS

NAME AND RELATIONSHIP TO PARENTS

_____

_____

ADVICE FOR PARENTS

_____

_____

_____

WISHES FOR BABY

_____

_____

_____

GUESTS

NAME AND RELATIONSHIP TO PARENTS

_____

_____

ADVICE FOR PARENTS

_____

_____

_____

WISHES FOR BABY

_____

_____

_____

GUESTS

NAME AND RELATIONSHIP TO PARENTS

_____

_____

ADVICE FOR PARENTS

_____

_____

_____

WISHES FOR BABY

_____

_____

_____

GUESTS

NAME AND RELATIONSHIP TO PARENTS

_____

_____

ADVICE FOR PARENTS

_____

_____

_____

WISHES FOR BABY

_____

_____

_____

GUESTS

NAME AND RELATIONSHIP TO PARENTS

_____

_____

ADVICE FOR PARENTS

_____

_____

_____

WISHES FOR BABY

_____

_____

_____

GUESTS

NAME AND RELATIONSHIP TO PARENTS

_____

_____

ADVICE FOR PARENTS

_____

_____

_____

WISHES FOR BABY

_____

_____

_____

GUESTS

NAME AND RELATIONSHIP TO PARENTS

_____

_____

ADVICE FOR PARENTS

_____

_____

_____

WISHES FOR BABY

_____

_____

_____

GUESTS

NAME AND RELATIONSHIP TO PARENTS

_____

_____

ADVICE FOR PARENTS

_____

_____

_____

WISHES FOR BABY

_____

_____

_____

GUESTS

NAME AND RELATIONSHIP TO PARENTS

_____

_____

ADVICE FOR PARENTS

_____

_____

_____

WISHES FOR BABY

_____

_____

_____

GUESTS

NAME AND RELATIONSHIP TO PARENTS

_____

_____

ADVICE FOR PARENTS

_____

_____

_____

WISHES FOR BABY

_____

_____

_____

GUESTS

NAME AND RELATIONSHIP TO PARENTS

_____

_____

ADVICE FOR PARENTS

_____

_____

_____

WISHES FOR BABY

_____

_____

_____

GUESTS

NAME AND RELATIONSHIP TO PARENTS

_____

_____

ADVICE FOR PARENTS

_____

_____

_____

WISHES FOR BABY

_____

_____

_____

GUESTS

NAME AND RELATIONSHIP TO PARENTS

_____

_____

ADVICE FOR PARENTS

_____

_____

_____

WISHES FOR BABY

_____

_____

_____

GUESTS

NAME AND RELATIONSHIP TO PARENTS

_____

_____

ADVICE FOR PARENTS

_____

_____

_____

WISHES FOR BABY

_____

_____

_____

GUESTS

NAME AND RELATIONSHIP TO PARENTS

_____

_____

ADVICE FOR PARENTS

_____

_____

WISHES FOR BABY

_____

_____

_____

GUESTS

NAME AND RELATIONSHIP TO PARENTS

_____

_____

ADVICE FOR PARENTS

_____

_____

_____

WISHES FOR BABY

_____

_____

_____

GUESTS

NAME AND RELATIONSHIP TO PARENTS

_____

_____

ADVICE FOR PARENTS

_____

_____

_____

WISHES FOR BABY

_____

_____

_____

GUESTS

NAME AND RELATIONSHIP TO PARENTS

_____

_____

ADVICE FOR PARENTS

_____

_____

_____

WISHES FOR BABY

_____

_____

_____

GUESTS

NAME AND RELATIONSHIP TO PARENTS

_____

_____

ADVICE FOR PARENTS

_____

_____

_____

WISHES FOR BABY

_____

_____

_____

GUESTS

NAME AND RELATIONSHIP TO PARENTS

_____

_____

ADVICE FOR PARENTS

_____

_____

WISHES FOR BABY

_____

_____

_____

GUESTS

NAME AND RELATIONSHIP TO PARENTS

_____

_____

ADVICE FOR PARENTS

_____

_____

_____

WISHES FOR BABY

_____

_____

_____

GUESTS

NAME AND RELATIONSHIP TO PARENTS

_____

_____

ADVICE FOR PARENTS

_____

_____

WISHES FOR BABY

_____

_____

_____

GUESTS

NAME AND RELATIONSHIP TO PARENTS

_____

_____

ADVICE FOR PARENTS

_____

_____

_____

WISHES FOR BABY

_____

_____

_____

GUESTS

NAME AND RELATIONSHIP TO PARENTS

_____

_____

ADVICE FOR PARENTS

_____

_____

_____

WISHES FOR BABY

_____

_____

_____

GUESTS

NAME AND RELATIONSHIP TO PARENTS

_____

_____

ADVICE FOR PARENTS

_____

_____

_____

WISHES FOR BABY

_____

_____

_____

GUESTS

NAME AND RELATIONSHIP TO PARENTS

_____

_____

ADVICE FOR PARENTS

_____

_____

_____

WISHES FOR BABY

_____

_____

_____

GUESTS

NAME AND RELATIONSHIP TO PARENTS

_____

_____

ADVICE FOR PARENTS

_____

_____

_____

WISHES FOR BABY

_____

_____

_____

GUESTS

NAME AND RELATIONSHIP TO PARENTS

_____

_____

ADVICE FOR PARENTS

_____

_____

_____

WISHES FOR BABY

_____

_____

_____

GUESTS

NAME AND RELATIONSHIP TO PARENTS

_____

_____

ADVICE FOR PARENTS

_____

_____

_____

WISHES FOR BABY

_____

_____

_____

GUESTS

NAME AND RELATIONSHIP TO PARENTS

_____

_____

ADVICE FOR PARENTS

_____

_____

_____

WISHES FOR BABY

_____

_____

_____

GUESTS

NAME AND RELATIONSHIP TO PARENTS

_____

_____

ADVICE FOR PARENTS

_____

_____

_____

WISHES FOR BABY

_____

_____

_____

GUESTS

NAME AND RELATIONSHIP TO PARENTS

_____

_____

ADVICE FOR PARENTS

_____

_____

_____

WISHES FOR BABY

_____

_____

_____

GUESTS

NAME AND RELATIONSHIP TO PARENTS

_____

_____

ADVICE FOR PARENTS

_____

_____

_____

WISHES FOR BABY

_____

_____

_____

GUESTS

NAME AND RELATIONSHIP TO PARENTS

_____

_____

ADVICE FOR PARENTS

_____

_____

_____

WISHES FOR BABY

_____

_____

_____

GUESTS

NAME AND RELATIONSHIP TO PARENTS

_____

_____

ADVICE FOR PARENTS

_____

_____

_____

WISHES FOR BABY

_____

_____

_____

GUESTS

NAME AND RELATIONSHIP TO PARENTS

_____

_____

ADVICE FOR PARENTS

_____

_____

_____

WISHES FOR BABY

_____

_____

_____

GUESTS

NAME AND RELATIONSHIP TO PARENTS

_____

_____

ADVICE FOR PARENTS

_____

_____

_____

WISHES FOR BABY

_____

_____

_____

GUESTS

NAME AND RELATIONSHIP TO PARENTS

_____

_____

ADVICE FOR PARENTS

_____

_____

_____

WISHES FOR BABY

_____

_____

_____

GUESTS

NAME AND RELATIONSHIP TO PARENTS

_____

_____

ADVICE FOR PARENTS

_____

_____

_____

WISHES FOR BABY

_____

_____

_____

GUESTS

NAME AND RELATIONSHIP TO PARENTS

_____

_____

ADVICE FOR PARENTS

_____

_____

_____

WISHES FOR BABY

_____

_____

_____

GUESTS

NAME AND RELATIONSHIP TO PARENTS

_____

_____

ADVICE FOR PARENTS

_____

_____

_____

WISHES FOR BABY

_____

_____

_____

GUESTS

NAME AND RELATIONSHIP TO PARENTS

_____

_____

ADVICE FOR PARENTS

_____

_____

_____

WISHES FOR BABY

_____

_____

_____

GUESTS

NAME AND RELATIONSHIP TO PARENTS

_____

_____

ADVICE FOR PARENTS

_____

_____

_____

WISHES FOR BABY

_____

_____

_____

GUESTS

NAME AND RELATIONSHIP TO PARENTS

_____

_____

ADVICE FOR PARENTS

_____

_____

_____

WISHES FOR BABY

_____

_____

_____

GUESTS

NAME AND RELATIONSHIP TO PARENTS

_____

_____

ADVICE FOR PARENTS

_____

_____

_____

WISHES FOR BABY

_____

_____

_____

GUESTS

NAME AND RELATIONSHIP TO PARENTS

_____

_____

ADVICE FOR PARENTS

_____

_____

_____

WISHES FOR BABY

_____

_____

_____

GUESTS

NAME AND RELATIONSHIP TO PARENTS

_____

_____

ADVICE FOR PARENTS

_____

_____

_____

WISHES FOR BABY

_____

_____

_____

GUESTS

NAME AND RELATIONSHIP TO PARENTS

_____

_____

ADVICE FOR PARENTS

_____

_____

_____

WISHES FOR BABY

_____

_____

_____

GUESTS

NAME AND RELATIONSHIP TO PARENTS

_____

_____

ADVICE FOR PARENTS

_____

_____

_____

WISHES FOR BABY

_____

_____

_____

GUESTS

NAME AND RELATIONSHIP TO PARENTS

_____

_____

ADVICE FOR PARENTS

_____

_____

_____

WISHES FOR BABY

_____

_____

_____

GUESTS

NAME AND RELATIONSHIP TO PARENTS

_____

_____

ADVICE FOR PARENTS

_____

_____

_____

WISHES FOR BABY

_____

_____

_____

Attach Keepsakes and Pictures

★ GIFT LOG ★

★ GIFT LOG ★

GIFT RECEIVED	GIVEN BY

GIFT RECEIVED

GIVEN BY

_____   _____

_____   _____

_____   _____

_____   _____

_____   _____

_____   _____

_____   _____

_____   _____

_____   _____

_____   _____

★ GIFT LOG ★

GIFT RECEIVED	GIVEN BY

★ GIFT LOG ★

GIFT RECEIVED	GIVEN BY

★ GIFT LOG ★

GIFT RECEIVED	GIVEN BY
_____	_____
_____	_____
_____	_____
_____	_____
_____	_____
_____	_____
_____	_____
_____	_____
_____	_____
_____	_____
_____	_____

★ GIFT LOG ★

GIFT RECEIVED	GIVEN BY

★ GIFT LOG ★

GIFT RECEIVED	GIVEN BY

★ GIFT LOG ★

GIFT RECEIVED	GIVEN BY

★ GIFT LOG ★

GIFT RECEIVED	GIVEN BY

GIFT RECEIVED

GIVEN BY

_____   _____

_____   _____

_____   _____

_____   _____

_____   _____

_____   _____

_____   _____

_____   _____

_____   _____

_____   _____

Made in the USA
Monee, IL
28 September 2023